Before Tangible; there was Intangible
Embracing the Journey into ill
was only a matter of time till...

BREAKING

A Poetic Journey PT 1

Angel Gail
BA MA EFT MBS

BALBOA.PRESS
A DIVISION OF HAY HOUSE

Balboa Press books may be ordered through booksellers or by contacting:

Balboa Press
A Division of Hay House
1663 Liberty Drive
Bloomington, IN 47403
www.balboapress.co.uk
UK TFN: 0800 0148647 (Toll Free inside the UK)
UK Local: (02) 0369 56325 (+44 20 3695 6325 from outside the UK)

Because of the dynamic nature of the Internet, any web addresses or
links contained in this book may have changed since publication and
may no longer be valid. The views expressed in this work are solely those
of the author and do not necessarily reflect the views of the publisher,
and the publisher hereby disclaims any responsibility for them.

The author of this book does not dispense medical advice or prescribe the use
of any technique as a form of treatment for physical, emotional, or medical
problems without the advice of a physician, either directly or indirectly. The
intent of the author is only to offer information of a general nature to help
you in your quest for emotional and spiritual well-being. In the event you use
any of the information in this book for yourself, which is your constitutional
right, the author and the publisher assume no responsibility for your actions.

Any people depicted in stock imagery provided by Getty Images are
models, and such images are being used for illustrative purposes only.
Certain stock imagery © Getty Images.

Print information available on the last page.

ISBN: 978-1-9822-8678-1 (sc)
ISBN: 978-1-9822-8679-8 (e)

Balboa Press rev. date: 12/30/2022

FOR FAMILY

Whether together or apart,
your always in my heart.
Through shine & rain.
No matter what pain.
Whether red, green, or blue
I WILL **ALWAYS** LOVE YOU.

3+3

Angel Gail ©

Contents

BREAKING...

*All poetry & text written & created by Angel Gail ©

Creator of letzgocreate.com

Forewords
The starts of Breaking...

I truly had no idea I had been struggling with mental, emotional & spiritual needs.

I believe that these 3 parts are like an egg; one part is not complete till all 3 are whole & together.

My life was a delicate egg, with parts & pieces starting to break. I have been mending the 3 parts ever since & now I know that the body can only truly heal when you have completed your egg.

Of course, beginning to break means that no-one can see it, we use every invisibility cloaking device we can think of. If possible, we slip so far out of sight we forget time and space can exist, instead, finding new ways to torcher ourselves is all too common.

It is the intangibility where most of the damage is done, we smile while we internally beat upon a small frail self that does not deserve such lack of respect. Sad to say humans do such a good job to plaster up the broken bits, apply tape, bandage, and extra dressings. Until it spills out from the inside to become very visible and tangible.

Anyone who has been in broken relationships, made poor choices, or had trauma in their lives knows to what I refer, we try so hard to keep it going, finding other such life type things to keep us focused and busy. This process of denial usually makes the situation far worse, however.

I guess it's a bit like being part of the omelette, you don't know if your cooked and its done till it's all ova !

I was now on my own, trying hard to figure life out again, mentally messed from a lifetime of traumas while attempting to be a single parent to 3 of various ages. I knew it wasn't going to be easy, as I had been avoiding this decision to enter a world of divorce, for a long, long time.

I wanted to write in a poetic gesture, my thoughts and feelings of the pre-diagnosis years leading up to the **"CRACKING"** point, which I finally reached sometime later. (Book Pt 2)

This is the first leg of a 13-year journey

I was a blathering messy pre-diagnosis
confusing mess.

I tried to keep composed,

but eventually the fake must be exposed.

Raw and wriggling,

It slowly manifested to

the surface.

THE SEED

This is the very **Essence of Life**
The cradle of existence.
The hope of all possibilities both
Known & Unknowable.
With this hope comes a spark
& With this spark…Is the perfection of
change, growth, love & pure thought.
For it is this life of a dormant space
& place, before the birthing of
a new leap forward.
Moving into the awakening of …
THE SEED
Angel Gail ©

BEFORE THE BREAKs

I Cried a Stream...

I had nothing left. My marriage came to a necessary end.
I cried out to God... BUT with no avail, in that
moment
I lost all that I was.
Foundations crumbled and I cried deeper and longer till
my soul broke in two.

I Cried a River...

I started again.

I found a path & cut a new way forward. Living a lone
parent-life, I became stronger than before.
One day, my right leg was dragging, next came the
numbness, I cried,
Could it be MND?
Could it be My 9yr old would be alone!?
Diagnosis & a year of tests & uncertainty followed.

NO TEARS CAME. Finally,

Diagnosis-Multiple Sclerosis & my body shut down.

I would cry in the morning...I would cry in the night...
I would cry when she left for school.... I
would cry with friends & I cried ALONE....
for my future & for the uncertainty.
I would cry "for what can I give my child now?."

I Cried an Ocean....

So many tears have been cried out from my soul.
The feeling was, its all too intense.
With all those tears I feel like I could drown.
I'm sure I can't have any left?

But now a new awakening, of self & understanding.
I'm ready to face a new dawn.
So I give my spare tears that I have left. Mine to yield,
it is a gift......No more tears for me to shed.

I Cried No More.

19 YEARS.... Fly right by.

When you are in it, no-one knows.
When your knee deep in mess no-one
gets it.
When your hips are sinking into the bog,
no-one sees it, and....

When you are finally drowning, it's up
to you to either puff up with hot air and
shout for help, or to fill your lungs with
fluid and drown.

It's not their fault, it's your choice,
Right or wrong, good, or bad, the power of
the voice is yours to command.

After all if you become mute! & your power
has been taken. Then finding it is also up
to you.

Of course, to put up a great façade is
usually what we humans do.

-Trapped
Packaged in white
    Wrapped in a veil
        Adorned with flowers
            Smothered with promises
                Trapped by a ring
            Witnessed by many
        Bound by paper
    Can't get out
    Nowhere to go
OBJECT OF LUST

Getting the box...

...Get in the box

...Get in the box!

Silently...

Unravelling

its perfection with time......

Time ticks by like a blink of an eye.....

19 years fly right by... S.O.S...

Save our souls...Sold our souls.

Facing my Fears
-A Trauma prayer

I

wanted so much to be brave.
Crumbling,
Whimpering,
Invisible to the naked eye…
I kept going it was a daily struggle.
One where I count every breath & every
step that I need to take.
One where without a ward of care by my
side I may most certainly have chosen a
darker option.
One where the light of day would not have
risen…..
So, I cried inside….

"Help me to face my deepest fears to pull out the tar of toxicity.
But above all of this….
an Abundance of forgiveness for,
I need to be freed."

Facing my Fears
A Trauma prayer

Help me to have the strength, my deepest fears to face.

The Courage inside to sculpt, to trace.

The Grace

To give myself time, with space.

For a life altering knowledge, I will embrace.

But above all of this....

The Abundance of forgiveness & Love, I need to create,

The wisdom to accept, to find a new fate.

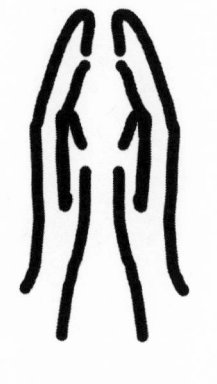

Guides from above

Till I am a fountain of light & pure love,

Eternally

Springing up from within.

Poetic Journey Part I

Introduction

Breaking ...

Tumbling into a void, where time slips away: the pre-post diagnosis years, spirals headlong into a zone of confusion, tears, tantrums & shadows.

I would find solace in the dark **black holes** of the mind that I didn't know existed.

Before Visible; there was Invisible
Before Tangible; there was Intangible

Before, it was only a matter of time till...

An Anger that had been dormant yet boiling beneath a façade was awakened. It was creating an MS pathway to pure destruction, that yet I did not fully understand.

I guess you could say I was in a very dark lonely space, a shadow land of sadness, grief & loss, I was responding pretty much like a 'self-torcher' victim might,(Shining a light inside) the inaudible voice inside my head immediately went into self-floggings acting as though I did not in any way shape or form deserve this pile of crap that was being dumped upon my lap nor was, I doing good enough.

Peering Inside the *Keyhole* hidden away from mass onlookers, was where I continued to suffer.

The blackness pouring in was slowly choking me & I knew in my soul that I had to find answers.

I had no idea where to look or what sort of help was required but I knew my mind foundations of what I had once stood on were once again being undermined.

What I could not imagine was what could possibly take its place, all I had ever understood was my own belief system that had been cultivated out of a broken trauma filled childhood. "Well, what's wrong with that?" I queried

Sometimes there is no other way than the most difficult of directions to take, a pathway if you were of sound mind you would never consider taking. I had to explore the darkness to want to reach for the light.

I was being told by the medical profession it's a **sick life** that I was signed up for now, one which I would have to conform to. I guess the rebel that is in us all the teenager eager to flee the nest to prove oneself is where my heart wanted to go, I found some solace in beaches **Where Angels Tread,** for a momentary peace to reset my '*fuzzed up*' head.

Soon after the diagnosis I found myself in a double whammy relapse. I lost my ability to structure sentences, I would often get stuck on letter pronunciation and certain key words were unavailable to my speech cortex, the letters M & F were a struggle, I would stammer unable to speak or think clearly. **MS & Can you see me?** can't talk, can't stand, can't walk, a tough year followed, as did the **Waves of emotions.**

Falls became a constant companion, as I broke multiple times these **rocky roads** became all I could see. The danger of falls became increasingly real.

The feeling of restraint and control by an external force was tightening in on my every fibre of being, the need for medication balancing the need for growth healing & finding alternative roads to walk, was being fought in a war with smiling faces, I became ***Breathless with anticipation*** someone must speak up or otherwise. what are we here for?

All that I could manage at this insane time during the darkest of days.
It was going to be ***1step @ a time....***

The POETIC journey begins....

BREAK
No 1

Keyhole

As I've already said, I was responding pretty much like a self-torcher (see above) victim might.

The inaudible voice inside my head wanted to go back to auto pilot of self-floggings, this was a viol behaviour yet not understood in any way shape or form. I berated the Me I thought I was meant to be, was I doing good enough?

I whipped myself momentarily, pausing for only gaps to breath, the berating was constantly on repeat for sure.

Peering Inside the Keyhole hidden away from mass onlookers, was where I hid & continued to suffer.

-KEYHOLE

Locked

Do you dare to look in?

For lost, painful memories lay within.

Torture yourself. . . . for you hold the key

But do you want to set yourself free?

Isn't it best to stay on the run?

Never look back . . . . Barely hold on.

Let the pains torments and play with your mind.

Till you believe . . . . It's you that's really unkind.

Allow it to torture and rot out your guts.

Until cancerous cells . . .EAT YOU ALL UP

BREAK No 2

Black-hole's, fill my eyes, invade my head
I **fu-king truly** wish that I was dead

Slow waster !? **F ...uckkkk that!**
That's not for me
I'm better off out of here
as quick as can be

Watch me melt slowly till I wither away

What choice do I have?

Is there not another way?

This is a total *funk* with my head
It's Christmas Day & . . .
I wish I was dead

Trainers & pyjamas & keys in hand
I'm *fun-king-off* to another land

Why should I stay to waste away?

What joy is there in...

one more
day?

Drown.   **Me.**   **Please.**

BREAK

No 3

A Sick Life

I had no idea where to look or what sort of help was required but I knew my mind foundations of what I had once stood on were once again being trashed like a house being bulldozed to rubble.

So I fumbled around with no direction,
No faith in the new me
&
No real grasp on reality.

I was being told by the medical profession it's a *sick life* that I was signed up for now.

one which I would have to conform to.

One where medication was supposed to dictate my life...

I disagreed most heartily.

Relentlessly I would be offered a multitude of opportunities to follow a drug-filled path.

Uneasy, my heart wept bitter tears for the me as she disappeared down a diagnosis tunnel.

All through her childhood & those dark years
Owned, controlled and full of fears
A yearning for an absent father appears.
With bravery and courage in both hands
She reached fourth and finds this man.
After 19 long years of separate
He is found & it seems so great.
The relationship blooms & the years that were
lost,
Shrink in memory, evaporate At NO cost?

The flawless timing of Fate....
Steps in to lend its cruel hand
She is stolen away to a distant land.
And once again he is removed from her side
Time spent together has been denied.
He suddenly becomes ill with MND
A violently volatile Neuro.... wasting disease.
MN-DEATH is the ONLY polite release.

From a distance she's held
By an unsympathetic man.
Now he's gravely ill, NO time to lose,

She journeys to reach for his outstretched arm
TOO LATE, remorseful is all that can be
The unfathomable loss and tragedy.

Years roll by and now she's free
From all control in HER society.

Only 3 years in count, she feels unwell,
Dragging HER leg is first to fell.
IGNORE! Best policy, it will go away.
She will live to fight another day.
Soon it becomes FAR too obvious.
She has no choice but to make a fuss.
She fears that it might be **MND**, OH GOD
…. don't be so ridiculous!

A year and a bit the diagnosis takes
lots of needles tests MRI's... but NO mistakes.
They offer up a list of possibilities
This does not reduce or make ease.
Finally, the table is set
A lifetime's choice for you to digest

"HERE YOU ARE
This is for you
Its Neuro-sister MS...
This is what you have, probably?
At best..."
SO TAKE THE TABLET....
SWALLOW THE PILL.
"From now on we'd like you to always be ill.
Our turn to OWN you.... add a bit more!
Drugs are so expensive…
your value just increased by four!"

"The side-effects well, they are not great,
But I'm sure we can find a way to **compensate**.*"*

"NO....
That's not for me & I will find....
another way to leave YOU behind
I have not fought to lose control
My future is

MY PRIZE

MY GOAL."

BREAK

No 4

Where Angel's Tread.

I guess the rebel that is in us all at some point must spill out.

The teenager who is eager to flee the nest, to prove oneself.

I wanted to leave and not know where I was going. Pack a bag, don't look back and not think about the mundane of bills, that's where my heart wanted to go.

As I searched my heart that night, feeling nothing but an empty-energy space, I was unable say or do anything to pump it up.

I crawled to bed & wept deep long tears.

The morning dawn found me with warm crisp sunshine, the car whisked me to the nearest gold nest, I found some solace on the beach **Where Angels Tread**....

And for a brief time I found a momentary peace to reset my *'funked-up'* head.

Whilst driving on the road one day,
an elderly man fell in my way,

His shoes were all that I could see.
I braked hard,

I stopped …

he lay …

he looked at me.
Shock set in on this man,
I flew to the side as fast as I can.

**Without a thought or concern of harm,
I stopped the traffic with my palm.**

Cars parted left and rights,
But no one stopped to see

if you ....
were alright!

The dignity & grace of this man,
was left lying on the ground.

I could not stand by while **others** ....
drove round.

"The man had fallen can't you see,
Where is your sense of humanity."

Oh, sympathy where have you gone,
Why is it that this seems so wrong.

It aches my heart to see it so,
Indeed it crushes to my soul.

Where is the sense of Fellow man
Where is the care to Lend a hand.

I need my space to clear my head.....

I need to be where angels tread.

Upon the beach then I shall go,

Give me peace

make me whole.

BREAK

No 5

Nothing but controlled.

I still struggled as I felt ***Nothing but controlled.*** Having no answers, no idea of who to turn to for guidance.

I was hearing tons of doctor advice, but it felt like nonsense to me.

·Nothing but control

I feel trapped; I feel taught
I feel horridly caught.

I feel moaned, as I've groaned,
I feel dreadfully owned.

Who's to say, who's to tell,
who's to make...give me hell.

Take the pill
Feel the trill
Do exactly what we say.

Can't you see ?

Can't you Guess?

What a horrible mess!

Well, I can tell & I can see
It's so obvious
...at least it is to me.

I just think... they can't sink any lower than they have
Yet in my eyes,
with no surprise.

Before I Know I'm on their drugs

Owned......

Moaned.....

&
  Full of Woe.

BREAK

No 6

...Can you see me?

Shortly after the diagnosis, I found myself in a double whammy relapse.

I lost my ability to structure sentences, I would forget words, names or often I would become stuck on letter pronunciation & certain key words were unavailable to my speech cortex.

The letters M & F were for some weird reason were the biggest struggle...
So I couldn't even cuss well,

I would stammer out words, unable to speak or think clearly.

There was an audible outpouring of the impediment I was starting to suffer.

This was mixed with a 'heady' dose of fear.

Fear of life, death, of the MS mess I clearly now was.

If I could exist as this?

Was I ever coming back?

&....Can you still see me ?

· Can you see me?

MS I'm a mess,MS I'm a mess,
I'M A MESS .... (whispered) I'm a mess I'm a mess,

MSMSMSMSMSMSMSMSMSMS

I'm a mess I'm a mess I'm a mess!!
MSMSMS . M. S.M.S.M.S.M.S.

Mmmmmmmmmm, Essssssssssss.
MS I'M A MESS, I'M A MESS, I'M A MESS, I AM A MESS....
I'm a mess, I'm a mess, I'm a mess !!
CAN YOU SEE ME ?

I mess, I mess, I miss I miss ... I miss ME
**For I'm not myself,
don't you see?**
m.s m.s m.s m.s I miss me

M.S I cry, I am Me?
.......This ME, Can YOU still see?

MS *M.S* *M.S* *M.S* ***A MESS***

71

BREAK

No 7

Waves of emotions.

I had a catastrophic loss of memory with a triple whammy of....

Can't think
Can't talk
Can't stand
Can't walk

A tough year followed as did the ***Waves of my Internal Emotions.***

Waves of emotion, waves roll in,
crashing in turmoil,
......as they crush in.

Sweet waves of emotion........
Your helter-skelter like patterns
roll in.

They tease me, torment me
into a turbulence spin.

Up-and-down I find they throw
I crash...
I spin...

I rise...
I fall

Bittersweet emotions
entwine all

Do not consume my breath...
my life
my soul

I rise above the waves.

BREAK

No 8

These Rocky Roads

Falls became a constant companion...

As I broke multiple times *these rocky roads*
became all I could see.

The danger of falls became more popular !
increasingly more frequent.

These rocky roads,
Oh, these Rocky paths......
they steal my feet from under me.
Unsure my foot becomes,
I find it trembles so.

My vision becomes clouded
for the way forward,
I no longer see clear.
Tears stream down,
for a while I become unsure.

Oh pebbles that slide in the mud
You make my path
so treacherous
I fear life itself

Rocky road
Rocky paths
you steal my feet
from under me.

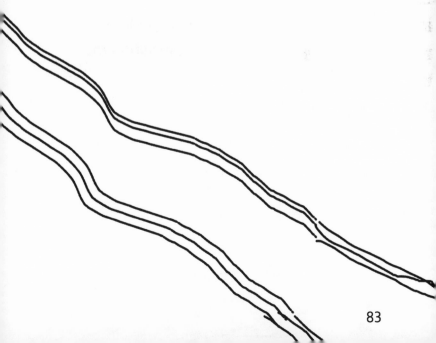

if I were to slip upon the stony ground
would I be forlorn
would someone lend an arm?

Dare I risk to move upon
dare I risk to travel on

For me the risk is so high
I travel light as I look to the sky

I need to keep you at arm's length

I need to find what gives me strength

BREAK

No 9

Raw Emotions.

The opening of my very *'Raw emotions'* was captured so utterly in these two words.

To say I was emotionally hurting as if skinned but still alive was as close as you could get to the truth.

> *"Sensations of the mind become sensations of the flesh"*

It was difficult to last one day at a time, I could feel the weight of the diagnosis bearing down on my shoulders with its unyielding blanketed grasp upon my throat.

As time began to move forward I remained stuck in the waiting line for the final, whatever ?
it was as if I were *so twisted in time.*

'A n d s e l f t o r t u r e d t h e y b e c o me.'

Sensations of the mind become
sensations of the flesh
holds a carnal knowledge of the
intimate self.

Black shadows engulf
the inky dank pit of our fears
our rejections
our pains
I conjure illusionary sensations
to fill up the gaps.

A past-long-lived–life-left far behind

Still coursing through my blood
as a river of sludge May.
Slowly
Unyielding
with its blanketed grasp upon my
throat

raw and renewed the memories stir
And yet
so twisted in time....

A n d s e l f t o r t u r e d t h e y b e c o m e

BREAK

No 10

Breathless with Anticipation
Q?

I was soooooooooo ANGRY
AND I was soooooooooo unhinged.

What does this mean, what can I do, be,
see, care, give a damn....

I barely notice I can't breathe, I've spent
my whole life in a sort of corset, so what's
the difference now?

If you don't give a rat's arse, why should I
be the voice of reason?

Where does it stop.
How does it stop.
Can it ever truly STOP?

-Breathless with
Anticipation

Q?
ComMANded
CONTAINED
CONSTRICTED
CONSTRUCTED
CONTROLLED
Please. . . CONFORM? (shouted)

DO-**MEN-**ATED
Dom-MEN-ants
GOVERN-MEN-T or GUIDEANCE?
MAN-AGE-MEN-T
MANipulation
Pre-Dom-MEN-Nation(shouted)

TIGHT strings….. NO loose things.
Puppetry & corsetry combined.

KEPT… In a box,
in a cage, behind bars,
Behind boning & wires.

(shout)
"OH, KEEPER" of the free thinker, philosopher & tinkers. Are WE toymakers to be.... JUST clinkers?

Is the sound to RESOUND like a gong in the sky.
Or to fall on deaf ears by the **'MAN'** placed on high.

(shouted)
NO I DON'T THINK SO. NOT time to conform. Strings to unravel & the confines of Restriction To ..... UN-UNIFORM.

I look here upon a SAD STATE of Affairs.
Where I see control staring back
At me
EVERYWHERE.

The 'MAN'
who hates,
who NEVER cares.
Pulls in SPITE …on my strings,
forcing me to….

(shouted)
**HOLD TIGHT AND
BREATHE IN!**

NOW is the time to awake
and be counted.

IF NOT…..We are sure to be
……found floundered.

(shouted)
**SO I charge each one of you
to pay good attention.**
Or LOST you will be….
With some self-

REPREHENSION.

BREAK

No 11

Charred heart

My heart was 100% burnt out.
I had managed to achieve this splendour
of annihilation in what was relevantly a
short period of my life, or so I thought, in
fact I had been doing damage for a much
longer period of time.

> *'Consumed by its melancholic rage,*
> *That twists in my mind*
> *. . . how it devours me.'*

I had previously thought that I was on
my game as I may have already said this
before now, & if am repeating, you can
take this, one of two ways it's either;

A point that needs to be re-enforced
Or forgotten.
For now, I'll leave that for you to decide!

\- **Charred heart**

Flames upon my wooden heart,
Blackened to the core.

Consumed by its melancholic rage,
That twists in my mind
. . . how it devours me.

Thy darkness,
Raging upon the flesh,
Manifests. . . .
and indifference to life.

Thy breath . . . shallow . . . & listless.
Distant smells of singe remains.

Tis' my Soul crying out,
in pain from the furnace,
still fevers in the fires,

Burnt out. . .
Despondent . . .
& dried out.

While it's cauterised shell has sealed it with. . .
A permanent resolute.

How doth an ember remain
When the flame long since died?

Could it be . . . a new fire,
will awaken?
Reigniting the flame of hope.

Free from dark form . . .
. . . free to live once more.

Charred Wooden Heart,
I charge the to try.

BREAK

No 12

#Onestep@atime....

The journey begins.

Sometimes there is no other way other than the most difficult of directions to take,

A pathway if you were of sound mind you would never consider taking.

I had to explore the darkness I found myself so utterly ruined by in order, to find what direction I would walk to reach for the light.

Sometimes, I guess...

like *Alice* you must tumble down a hole to find yourself.

All that I could manage at this insane time during the darkest of days, was to fall, tumble & get back up.

it was going to be

1step @ a time....

My own personal journey

was about to begin.

- One step at a time....

Each day I put one foot on the floor.
Each repetitive monotonous day I walk forward,
the numb sensation....
Lifting the dragging dead object,
I know longer recognise as mine.
Emotionally unstable I fall,

I say . . . . *"One step at a time."*

Blackness engulfs the mind,
invades my space
. . . Gnarled & twisted.
It gives me no rest for I am truly wicked,

I tell myself . . . ***"One step at a time."***

The Journey is effort,
lifting my head...
To roll out of bed,
Seems impossible some days.
The vision dangerous & blurred,
still I push with all my might,
to clear the haze.
I think,

"Just one more .... one step at a time"

I lumber with great difficulty,

to clamber down the moving stairs.

I ask "Is this day even possible?"

Hope dwindles,

I become my own living darkness.

I shriek aloud,

"One step at a time . . . that's all I can do."

BREAK

No 13

A Ray of Light

A Spark was all I needed to light a fire that had been left in ashes.

The phoenix sprung to mind as I dwelt on life as I now know it.

Holding tight with all my might, I sent a simple prayer to somewhere up there;

"Oh PLEASE...

Help Me

Find a Better Way"

-A Ray of light

Till I talked I didn't know
What
was trapped inside
I was left with no excuses
Nowhere to Hide.

A Ray of light shone in &
showed me The way
With Time
Effort & Truth
I'm ready to face anew day.

This Ray of light, gave to me...
a renewed direction
With Courage, Hope
& some Thought Correction.

The solace of suicide
how it could not stay
Offering me grace
to find a brighter day.

Thankyou
my Ray of light.

Daily Confirmations of Affirmations

PLANTING OUR SEEDS

Even though I am breaking
& I feel in a mess...
I begin to understand there is a SEED of
New-Beginning's.
As yet I don't understand why
I am not growing?
& still, I completely deeply accept
that something needs to change...
I want to grow, so I must learn.
I need to find **Self-Love**,
I need to figure how to **Forgive**.
Even though my heart is heavy & I am
only a **Small Seed of Thought.**
I wish nothing more than to
develop into more.
Therefore, I truly **deeply &
completely** wish to find ways that
I can learn to accept who I am.
**Love who I am & forgive all things
I need to**.

BREAKING

Is the starting point of this
memorable
13 year journey.
Part 1 leads on to...

Part1·5
Poetic memoirs
BREAKING MY EGG

Before Visible; there was Invisible
As the truth is revealed
so too is a new Journey

BREAKING
MY EGG

PT1 · 5 Poetic Memoirs

Angel Gail BA MA EFT MBS

INTRODUCTION

BREAKING MY EGG

Excerpt From bk1.5

Breaking my egg.

Tumbling into a void, where time slips away: the pre-post diagnosis 4 crazy years, spirals headlong into a zone of confusion, tears, tantrums & shadows.

I truly had no idea I had been struggling with the 'old black dog', but as I unravelled so did the depression, anxiety and want for a suicidal sleep.

In fact, plans unhatched in my sleep, in my daymares, all the time I was thinking, I was contemplating existence and the point of it!

As I entered the domain of illness, only to find that the biggest illness was that of my mind, my thought processing was ill. I had in truth, no idea that there was any mental disturbance going on inside.

Life is full of twists and turns, none of which make much sense at the time. I suppose we all try to figure out the best way we can.

As for myself, I had dedicated most of my life to my own family, working with a vast variety of children and care work style jobs in a multiple array of ages, as well as being a full-time mum to three.

Looking after others is easy right? To my thinking at that time was that my grasp on *'self'* was in a relatively good place & that my outlook on life was quite healthy, or so I thought.

•Mind• Bodily •Spiritual needs.

-A Trauma prayer

Help me to have the strength, my deepest fears to face.

The Courage inside to sculpt, to trace….

Chapter 1……..I had been putting my life back together over a long period of time, following a divorce, now living with debt, mortgage & home life with three children. I was building a new life for us, DIYing, learning to drive, & growing into bigger pants.

Now holding down two jobs, I embarked on balancing going back to school! A university BA in the study of fine Art part time. This was a task I had always wanted to try, one I never thought I could achieve due to lack of self-belief & fear of failure………

Moving to a new house was the next mission, a sort of cathartic clean break for me & my family.

As I finished clearing all debt from the past relationship, I was able to re-group. & with this new start came a burst of bravery.

Beginning to get ill during the house moving process, I questioned life all over again, So, with a mix of trepidation & courage in both hands, I seek a medical opinion, while loaded with a few questions in mind, but instead of reassurance's, to my dismay the doctor heard my pains & fears.

He was responding so fast that my world just spun fully out of control. I lost all sense of grounding with a sudden need for retreating to home hastily.

The Grace
To give myself time, with space.
For a life altering knowledge, I will embrace.

Chapter2 ....

A year of specialists followed with bloods, scans, MRI's & more bloods & finally a diagnosis in the summer at the same time wedding plans had been in full swing, that same month as I received my diagnosis my first born, my boy became a married man.

For myself keeping a smile on my fake face was all I could do, my heart wanted to tell my news but instead I was keeping this epiphany to myself.

I had one more part to wait for & that was the enjoyable task of a lumber puncture, with my heart still running on empty, I was informed by the specialists, this would very likely be 6-12 months waiting list It was absolutely from here on, all that I could comprehend to do was live life 1 step at a time.

But above all of this....

The Abundance of forgiveness & Love, I
need to create,
The wisdom to accept, to find a new fate.

Chapter 3...

To begin with I was so scared of being in
charge, that a vehicle was a mammoth
meal to swallow down, each month
that past I improved, & with each task
I accomplished my self-belief started to
improve too.
I started to see myself as fit for purpose,
no longer the useless bag of crap that I had
been led to believe I was.
I made lists in my head.

- I can do it.
- I want to move forward.
- I will be ok.
- Stay focussed.
- PS. Love yourself. Urrrrrggg!

Small steps, I know, but the bravery was
in there I just needed to believe it. I kept

finding ways to adjust myself growth, the next thing I did was realise I was on my own!? I know that sounds stupid, but it was only me that was going to see me through to a new happier future, after all id contemplated other options before now & not been brave/crazy enough to do it.

During my marriage I had come close on a few occasions to using alternative methods of leaving him, but all of them would have left my children with no mother.

Instead, I reached for a future, good or bad, right, or wrong I would try to stay brave.

Looking at the cards I made for my son to get through his school exams that he had been struggling with {no surprise mind you, home life had been HELL on EARTH}.

I viewed the set of four cards with fresh eyes, I read the words again & again.

1. What do you want?
2. How much do you want it?
3. What are you prepared to do?
4. {again}Stay Focused!

I figured, "I think it's time to make some plans". With pen & paper in hand I wrote my first list of future hopes, it looked something like this.

- Pass my 2part driving test
- Get a car
- Clear the debt
- Get a 2nd job
- Buy new clothes.

My list was a plan, so I put it on my bedroom draws & crossed all of my arms, fingers, toes &

eyeballs. Looking suitably like a cross between a ventriloquist puppet & a Yoga Master.

I wasn't sure if it would work but figured the only way from rock bottom was up, I guess?

I know there's lots worse off than I was, I still had a roof over our heads, my kids & I were managing to sort out life be it all a bit stressy-messy {technically not a real word but its staying in}.

I wasn't aware I was meant to be grateful, at times I was truly grateful but at other times I was plunging back into the darkness of despair. If things went wrong, I would go into panic internally.

…With Guides from above
Till I am a fountain of light & pure love.

Chapter 4...

I guess the rebel that is in us all, the teenager eager to flee the nest to prove oneself.
wanted to leave and not know where I was going. Pack a bag, don't look back and not think about the mundane of bills, that's where my heart wanted to go.

As I searched my heart that night, feeling nothing but an empty-energy space, I was unable say or do anything to pump it up.
I crawled to bed & wept deep long tears.

The morning dawn found me with warm crisp sunshine, the car whisked me to the nearest gold nest & I found some solace on the beach **Where Angels Tread,** for momentary peace to reset my fuzzed-up head.

....Eternally
Springing up from within.

Chapter 6....

MS...Can you see me?

Shortly after the diagnosis, I found myself in a double whammy relapse.
I lost my ability to structure sentences...
I would often get stuck on letter pronunciation...
certain key words were unavailable to my speech cortex.

The letters M & F were for some weird reason the biggest struggle so I couldn't even cuss well.
I would stammer unable to speak or think clearly.

There was an outpouring of the impediment I was suffering, mixed with a 'heady' dose of fear.

Fear of ... life, death, of the MS mess
I clearly now was.

If I could exist as this?

Was I ever coming back?

&.... *Can you still see me?*

BREAKING MY EGG...
Introduction

IS, the first in a series of memoir & poetry books opening the journey to the pre-diagnosis life on the edge of BREAKING. It is shared out over a 13year journey in easy-to-follow chunks.

They walk the path that Angel trod to find her own *'Journey less travelled'*.

When all on the outside looked fine but the intangible of the situation was a calm moving façade of fakery.

Suicide seamed a sane option, in fact the only real sensible thing to do! right?

….. The fact of the matter is, you are sure you are doing your family a kindness, you are being selfless by saving them from the **drama-lama** heading down a dark one-way street to pure blackness. Your head is so royally *funked-up* that this is the best idea you have ever had.

further truth still, it wasn't the first time I had stared down the barrel of this loaded gun.
I had been here in my teens when the dark shades had drawn a veil over my eyes before.

The true damage was internally hard-wired into the brain's invisible circuitry.

Sad to say it had been that way most of my life.

It was painfully clear that without a bolt of lightning or a series of unpleasant events, there would be no waking this gal up. Shock was her only hope.

If we as humans, could but see the crazy amounts of damage that we were pouring into our veins via bad life choices, words, actions & deeds,
maybe….
If we as soul-beings, also knew there was a cost to pay for these things, then just maybe we wouldn't stack up such a debt upon our younger selves?

After all, in our youth we may have had better ideas but just lost them on route somewhere.

I would like to think that we all would choose the more noble enlightened journey, if only someone would simply shine a light on such a road.

Either way the shock that I had been trying to avoid explodes inward.

Finding new thoughts was my only sensible option, as I started to question the existences of what I was living.

These are the dialogs of life as a newly found single parent.
I had to figure out debt, bills, & learn an array of new skills. Sinking or swimming were my only two main options.
I was as I say mum of 3 children.
No1 son was sweet 16
No2 daughter was just +13
No3 daughter was teeny weeny 3.3

In Short

A Journey 2 BREAKING
pre-post Diagnosis
Of How I CRACK to become an MS-MESS
How I discovered my full Mind-Madness
How/if you can Prevent or MEND?
Follow the trail to find out
How I did it ?
& WHY?

·Life's Ride

All that joined me on this
rollercoaster ride
had parts to play by my side.

It's the memoirs of a parent that
echo
Throughout
The people with parts, all get a shout
But the names are changed so
You don't know NOWT.

Please take a step on to the wild side
Help me un-cook a brain deep-fried
I hope you will join me
On this crazy
Ride.

All poetry in this book is original conjured, created &
written by Angel Gail ©

About the Author

Angel Gail has been on a 13-year journey of self-discovery.

Part1 of this Poetic Dialog takes place over a 4 year period, as life is starting anew. Here, in the darkness of the intangible, the sleeper is awakening.

Join Angel to unravel the mystery of who she really is verses who she thinks she is.

Letzgocreate A Room to Grow & Expand
Personal Notes.....

Personal Notes ...

The future is yours to create & command...
So write it well.